PAULIST BIBLE STUDY PROGRAM

Jesus and the Gospels

WORKBOOK

Workbook by   Kate Dooley, O.P. and Anne Dalton
Video Scripts by   Anthony Marinelli
Prayers by   Rea McDonnell, S.S.N.D.

PAULIST PRESS

New York/Mahwah

Acknowledgements

Cover photo: The Church of the Beatitudes. Courtesy of the Israel Government Tourist Office.

Interior photographs courtesy of the Israel Government Tourist Office and Lawrence Boadt, C.S.P.

Faith Sharing Principles are reprinted from RENEW, copyright © 1987 by the Roman Catholic Archdiocese of Newark, New Jersey. Used by permission.

Published by Paulist Press
997 Macarthur Blvd.
Mahwah, NJ 07430

Printed and bound in the United States of America.

Dear Friends,

It is a pleasure to present our new Paulist Bible Study Program. The Paulist Bible Study Program is designed to help adults understand the Bible in the light of contemporary biblical scholarship and to use the Bible as a source of prayer, reflection and action. It relates the study of the Bible to the liturgy, to the church, and to our daily lives. Those who long to know more about the Bible, based on the authentic Catholic tradition and the most responsible and best biblical scholarship, have a rich experience awaiting them.

Kevin A. Lynch, C.S.P.
Publisher

INTRODUCTION

Welcome to the Paulist Bible Study Program and to this first unit on the New Testament.

In this unit you will be introduced to the study of the New Testament and to the gospels of Matthew, Mark and Luke. This Workbook will serve as a reading guide to the Bible and to your companion text *Reading the New Testament* by Pheme Perkins. Each week it will point out what passages of the Bible you should read and what parts of the companion text are focused on these passages.

The Bible in the Life of the Church

The emergence of popular interest in the Bible among Catholics stems from the Second Vatican Council. Along with the new emphasis on the Scriptures during the Eucharist and other sacramental celebrations, the Council called upon all members of the church to grow in their knowledge and love of the Bible:

> Just as the life of the church grows through persistent participation in the eucharistic mystery, so we may hope for a new surge of spiritual vitality from intensified veneration for God's word (*Decree on Revelation*, 26).

The vision of the central place of the Scriptures which the Council set forth is becoming more and more a reality.

The church has always venerated the divine Scriptures just as she venerates the body of the Lord, since from the table of both the word of God and of the body of Christ she unceasingly receives and offers to the faithful the bread of life, especially in the sacred liturgy. She has always regarded the Scriptures together with sacred tradition as the supreme rule of faith, and will ever do so. (*Decree on Revelation,* 21.)

Our hope is that this program will be yet another resource which will take the process of integrating Scripture into the life of the Church one step further.

Jesus' Own Bible Study Model

In 1986, Archbishop Roger Mahoney of Los Angeles issued a pastoral letter entitled "The Bible in the Life of the Church." One part of the letter reflects on Jesus' own approach to teaching the Scriptures to his disciples as he walked with two of them on the road to Emmaus (Luke 24:13-35). Archbishop Mahoney's reflections on this passage are a fitting introduction to our study of the Bible.

The two disciples are on their way from Jerusalem to Emmaus when Jesus—his appearance hidden—joins them. He responds to their bewilderment by "interpreting for them every passage of Scripture which referred to him." This was the most clear example of Jesus sharing the Scriptures that we find in the gospels. For our own Bible study to be beneficial, then, we too must open our hearts and lives to allow Jesus to unlock the meaning of his message for us.

But two additional elements in the Emmaus journey are also required to validate our own experience of the Scriptures. First, our Scripture study must lead towards, center around, and flow from the Eucharist—the Mass. It was only in "the breaking of the bread" that the full meaning of Jesus' explanations became clear to the two men journeying to Emmaus. As Catholics, we too must always focus our Bible studies in and through the Eucharist. And secondly, we must be guided in our Scripture studies through "Simon Peter—the church." Recall that the two men returned in haste to Jerusalem where they were greeted with: "The Lord has been raised!It is true!He has appeared to Simon." This validation by Peter—by the church—is essential to our authentic understanding of the word of God.

The Importance of Commitment

What are your goals for your participation in this program? As you begin, take a few moments to reflect upon your goals and jot them down. These may involve gaining some knowledge, but don't omit other possible gains such as growing in your spirituality or prayer life, building community within your parish. Any goal worth achieving requires commitment. During this program you are invited to make a commitment to grow in your understanding and appreciation of the Bible.

All commitments require time. In this case, you are committing yourself to be present at the eight sessions and to participate in the learning process. This will require the most precious of commodities: time.

What follows is a description of the various steps you should take to prepare for and to follow-up on a meeting. Only you can determine how much time you have to spend on these steps. Not everything needs to be done now. Hopefully, the Paulist Bible Study Program will provide you with the resources to continue your own study well after a particular unit ends.

In addition to a time commitment, you are making a commitment to the other participants in your group. You bring unique gifts and experience to this study of the Bible that will enrich your co-learners. The steps below offer some tips on how you can both share your own insights and enable others to share theirs.

Preparing for the Meeting

Each week you will be meeting with others to reflect on the Scriptures and the parts of the companion text. Before you engage in the exercises in this book, follow the steps outlined for each session in the section called Preparation.

1. Prayerfully read the appointed Bible passages.

2. Read the assigned portion of the companion text. You may want to read a little bit each day to coordinate with your prayerful reading of the Bible. Many find it helpful to mark the text for key parts or to jot down questions that may arise during a reading.

3. Read the Focus and Review of Contents before the meeting. If you have time, try to work on responses to the review questions. Your companion text also has review questions after each chapter which will be helpful.

During the Meeting

Each session is designed to last two hours. Here are the steps for each session and some suggestions on how to make use of them.

Opening Prayer (5 minutes)
Place yourself and your group in God's presence, asking for the guidance of the Holy Spirit during the upcoming session.

Review of Contents (25 minutes)
This section gives you the opportunity to express what you have learned and to learn from the insights of others. If you have questions other than those raised in the review, bring them up at this time. While your Program Leader cannot be ex-

pected to have all the answers, he or she may be able to help you find an answer to your question.

Video (20 minutes)
The video is designed to enrich your learning by providing the visual dimension of what you are studying. Before viewing the program, look at the highlight questions. Jot down the answers as you watch the program. Afterwards, there is a brief time for your to raise questions or make a comment.

Learning Activity (25 minutes)
During this segment, you will work with others in an exercise to further integrate the meaning of the Scripture you have read and to apply it to your life.

Faith Sharing (25 minutes)
The following suggestions, borrowed from RENEW, are helpful guidelines for faith sharing:

• The entire faith-sharing process is seen as prayer, i.e., listening to the word of God as broken by others' experience.
• Constant attention to respect, honesty and openness for each person will assist the group's growth.
• Each person shares on the level where he/she feels comfortable.
• Silence is a vital part of the total process of faith sharing. Participants are given time to reflect before any sharing begins, and a period of comfortable silence might occur between individual sharings.
• Persons are encouraged to wait to share a second time until others who wish to do so have contributed.
• The entire group is responsible for participating and faith sharing.
• Confidentiality is essential, allowing each person to share honestly.
• Reaching beyond the group in action and response is essential for the growth of individuals, the group and the church.

Closing Prayer (10 minutes)
Having shared our faith together, we conclude with prayer. Join in the spirit of the prayer service by singing, praying, and listening to the word of God.

After the Meeting

Journaling
For each session, one or more journal idea is suggested. You may wish to keep a journal either to do these exercises, or simply to write your own reflections.

Additional Resources
Each week a number of sources are referred to for further reading and study. Your parish may have purchased these books for a parish resource library or you may obtain them from Paulist Press. Your program leader has further information. You may wish to consult these sources for continued study after the unit ends.

1. What is the New Testament?

FOCUS

We each bring our own personal level of understanding to the study of the New Testament. In this session we will get an overview of the New Testament books and look at the different types of writing found there. We will also explore the meaning of the Scriptures for our lives today.

OPENING PRAYER

Song Refrain:
"Grant to us, O Lord" by Lucien Deiss

or

Spoken Antiphon:
Open our hearts, Holy Spirit, to hear and rejoice in your word.

Reading
A reading from the prophet Jeremiah (31:31-34)

Song refrain or spoken antiphon

Prayer

Song refrain or spoken antiphon

GETTING STARTED

The New Testament has twenty seven books:

Four gospels grouped together at the beginning
The Acts of the Apostles
Thirteen letters, either written by Paul or attributed
to him
    Paul's letters have a set form:
    Greeting
    Short prayer
    Teaching addressing some problem within the
      community
    Exhortation to live a Christian way of life
    Farewell and short blessing
Epistle to the Hebrews
The seven letters attributed to the apostles
The Book of Revelation

The Sea of Galilee and Galilean hillsides.

LEARNING ACTIVITY

Put a check next to the statement which comes closest to describing your understanding of the gospels.

_____ 1. The gospels are biographies of all that Jesus did and said when he was on earth.

_____ 2. The gospels are written records of the preaching of the disciples about Jesus in the light of the resurrection. They take into account the mind set, the concerns, and the culture of the listeners.

_____ 3. The gospels are narratives about the words and actions of Jesus and what they mean for people today.

_____ 4. The gospels are part of a cultural inheritance and have importance because they have shaped Western thought and values.

BREAK

(10 minutes)

VIDEO

An introduction to the books and study of the New Testament.

As you view the video, please make note of the following:

1. What are the four kinds of criticism described in the program?

1. _____

2. _____

3. _____

4. _____

2. What are the three stages of the formation of the gospels?

1. _____

2. _____

3. _____

FAITH SHARING

1. How is Scripture a part of your daily life?

2. Read the Parable of the Sower (Mark 4:1-9) silently and then listen as your leader or another member of the group reads it aloud.

3. Give two or three words to describe these images:

footpath

rocky ground

thorns

good soil

4. Which of these images best represents the obstacles you face to hearing the word of God?

5. "Let those who have ears to hear me, hear!" What do you think it means to hear?

CLOSING PRAYER

A Call to Remember

All:
Now to God, who is able to accomplish far more than all we can ask or can even imagine, by the power at work within us, to God be glory in the church and in Christ Jesus for all generations, forever and ever. Amen.

Gospel

(All stand, holding tapers and facing the large candle at the center of the group.)

Reader:
The Good News of Jesus Christ, raised and with us here!

(Everyone now lights their tapers from the large candle and then listens to an adaptation of Luke 24:13-24.)

Concluding Prayer

All:
Our Mother and Father who art in heaven . . . . For the kingdom, the power and the glory are yours, now and forever. Amen.

Leader:
Let us go in peace to love and serve the Lord.

All:
Thanks be to God.

Song

FOLLOW-UP

A. Journaling

Read the parable of the sower and the seed, Mark 4:1-9.

What part of your life is the path that is beaten down?

Where is the rocky soil in your life?

What are the thorns that exist?

Do you recognize and can you identify the good soil in yourself?

Which of the obstacles to hearing the word of God do you need to overcome? What can you do to accomplish this?

B. Additional Resources

1. Read: Pheme Perkins, *Reading the New Testament*, Chapter 1, "Why Study the Bible," pp. 1-22.

2. Read: Anthony Marinelli, *Understanding the Gospels*, Chapter 1, "Formation of the Gospels," pp. 3-14.

3. Read: Raymond E. Brown, S.S., *Responses to 101 Questions on the Bible*, Questions 38-44.

4. Read: *The Catholic Study Bible*, "The Bible in Catholic Life," RG 16-30.

2. The Life of Jesus

Preparation

- Read Perkins, Chapter 3, "The Life of Jesus."

- Try to read as many of the references mentioned in the text as you can find time for. The following will be the focus of learning activities in this session:

    Miracle stories (cf. pp. 52-54 of the text)
    Mark 1:23-28 (exorcisms)
    Matthew 8:28-34
    Mark 6:30-44 (feeding the crowds)
    Mark 8:1-10
    Matthew 8:5-13 (healing)

    Pronouncements (cf. pp. 55-57 of the text)
    Mark 7:24-30
    Matthew 5:21-28

    Teaching (cf. pp. 67-68 of the text)
    Mark 2:23-28
    Mark 7:15
    Luke 6:27-36
    Luke 4:18-21

- Reflect on the FOCUS statement and REVIEW OF CONTENTS Questions.

FOCUS

Most of what we know about Jesus comes to us from the gospels. The gospels, however, do not give us an historical account of Jesus' life, as we understand history today. They are not modern-style biographies. On the other hand, the gospels do contain remembrances of Jesus' words and actions.

In seeking Jesus through the gospels, it is very helpful to understand how the gospels came to be. Much of what is contained in the gospels as we have them was originally handed on from community to community of believers *orally*. Stories were told of Jesus' miracles. His sayings were collected as his followers remembered them. The circumstances of his death were also recalled. All of these remembrances about Jesus were interpreted in the light of who the first Christians experienced Jesus to be: a turning point in their lives, the One who brought salvation, the Son of God. So, the life of Jesus that we read in the gospels is told through the eyes of faith. What was finally written down was what the first communities of Christians remembered and came to understand about the meaning (not just the facts) of Jesus' life, death, and resurrection.

OPENING PRAYER

Psalm 81

Left Side:
Shout with joy to God our defender!
Sing praise to the God of Israel!
Start the music, play the tambourine,
play pleasant music on harps and lyres,
blow the horn for the festival.

Right Side:
This is the law in Israel,
the command from our God.
God commanded this when God marched out on our
    behalf,
setting us free from slavery.

Leader:
Listen, my people, to me!
Oh my people, how I wish you would listen to me!
You must never worship another God.
It is I who led you from slavery.
Open your mouth and I will feed you.
I would feed you with the finest wheat
and satisfy you with honey.

All:
We open our ears and mouths and hearts and minds
tonight, our God, as best we can. Thank you for freeing
us from so many burdens that we might listen to the
good news more eagerly, more openly, with music in our
hearts. We pray this through Christ our Lord. Amen.

REVIEW OF CONTENTS

1. The early disciples of Jesus did not use writing to remember stories about him. In order to aid their memory they fitted many of the stories into forms or patterns that were already common in their culture.

a. What are the three components of the pattern of an exorcism story? (Check Perkins, p. 53)

b. Examine Matthew 8:28-34. Identify the three components.

Despite the fact that this story of the exorcism of demons by Jesus is similar in pattern to other exorcism stories (see that told by Perkins, pp. 52-53), are there any significant differences?

2. Read Mark 6:30-44 and Mark 8:1-10.

a. What are the similarities between these two accounts of Jesus' feeding a large number of people?

b. What evidence do scholars have for suggesting that these are two different versions of the same event? (Note chapter 8, verse 4. Do the disciples seem to have experienced a similar happening before?)

c. If these are not two different events, how does one explain the differences between the accounts? (See Perkins, p. 54)

3. Comparing accounts of events in Jesus' life as they are told by different evangelists often gives us clues to the "faith context," that is, the particular problems or needs of individual Christian communities. Preachers or missionaries adapted details of the story to suit these needs without changing the essential message or spirit of Jesus' life.

Review Mark 7:24-30 and Matthew 15:21-28, as compared by Perkins on pp. 56-57.

a. Identify the pattern of a pronouncement story (p. 55).

b. Note the differences in detail. What do these differences tell us about the community in which Matthew's version was preserved? (p. 57)

4. Jesus' followers experienced in their association with him that a new age of salvation was breaking into the world. Jesus' teachings often reflect the radical nature of this new age.

What does each of the following teachings of Jesus suggest about the kind of new age the first Christians experienced in Jesus? (See Perkins, pp. 67-68)

    Mark 2:23-28
    Mark 7:15
    Luke 6:27-36
    Luke 4:18-21

VIDEO

The World of Jesus and the Gospels.

As you view the video, make note of the following:

Who were:

Pharisees _____

Sadducees _____

Essenes _____

Zealots _____

Samaritans _____

BREAK

(10 minutes)

LEARNING ACTIVITY

The Gospels are witnesses to the faith experience of the first Christians. Jesus brought them new life. The demons of the old life were being cast out. The power of God was manifested in a new way.

Choose one of the following "first Christians." (Your leader may assign one to your group.) Then read the appropriate New Testament passages.

Peter
Luke 5:1-11
Matthew 10:1-5
Matthew 14:22-33
Matthew 16:13-16
Luke 22:54-62
Acts 2 (esp. 40-41)

Mary Magdalene
Luke 8:1-3
Luke 7:36-50 (which may refer to Mary Magdalene)
Matthew 27:56, 61
Mark 16:1
John 20:1-18

The Samaritan Woman
John 4:4-42

Nicodemus
John 3:1-21
John 7:50-51

Mary, Jesus' Mother
Luke 1:34-38
Luke 1:46-55
John 19:25-27
Acts 1:12-14

1. Make a note of and discuss

a. the nature of the person's first recorded encounter with Jesus

b. how that person's life was touched and changed by Jesus

c. any indication of the further effect that person's experience of Jesus had on others

2. Relying on your reading and review of Perkins, the video presentation, the specific New Testament references you have just read, and your imagination, construct a profile of your New Testament character. Have one of your group deliver it as a testimony. For example, you would begin, "I am Peter (or Mary, etc.) . . ." and proceed to tell his or her story.

FAITH SHARING

1. Reflect for a moment on the testimonies of New Testament Christians that you have just heard. Which of these first Christians (if any) appeals to you most? Why?

2. As was the case with the New Testament Christians you read about, Jesus' power works differently for different people. For Peter, it was gradual, with some major setbacks. For the Samaritan woman, it was more dramatic and immediate. How do you experience Jesus' presence in your life?

The Synagogue in Capernaum. Capernaum was the focus of much of Jesus' early ministry. These remains date from the third century A.D.

CLOSING PRAYER

A Call to Remember

Response:
Lord Jesus, thank you for yourself, for your Spirit, a fountain of living water springing up from deep within us. Please keep opening us to the depths of yourself, our self, the depths of your salvation, and our discipleship. We pray in the company of your first disciples:

Litany

Leader:	*All:*
Peter,	Pray with us.
Mary Magdalene,	Pray with us.
Nicodemus,	Pray with us.
Mary of Nazareth,	Pray with us.
Syrophoenician woman,	Pray with us.

(Add your own favorite New Testament disciples)

Leader:
Lord Jesus,

All:
Pray with us.

All:
Our Father and Mother, who art in heaven . . . . For the kingdom and the power and the glory are yours, now and forever. Amen.

Prayer

Leader:
Let us go in peace to love and serve the Lord.

All:
Thanks be to God!

FOLLOW-UP

A. Journaling

Think again of Jesus clashing with the demons and over-coming them. Mary Magdalene is described as a disciple from whom seven demons had been cast out. Write a prayer or reflection in which you acknowledge the modern demons that affect your life. Imagine your life without the influence of these demons. Are there steps you can take to live in such a new age of salvation initiated by Jesus?

B. Additional Resources

1. Read: Pheme Perkins, *Reading the New Testament,* Chapter 1, "The World of Jesus," pp. 23-50.

2. Read: Anthony Marinelli, *Understanding the Gospels,* Chapter 2, "The New Testament World," pp. 15-31.

3. Read: *The Catholic Study Bible,* "Introduction to the Synoptic Gospels," RG 386-388.

4. Using the Hammond *Atlas of the Bible Lands,* examine the maps on pages 24-25. Locate Palestine and Jerusalem on the map of the Roman world. What is Palestine called? What is its status with regard to Rome? Approximately how far is it from Jerusalem to Rome?

3. The Preaching of Jesus

Preparation

- Read Perkins, Chapter 4, "The Preaching of Jesus."
- Read as many of the following references in chapter 4 of the companion text as you can find time for:

Matthew 5:33-37	Mark 4:26-32
5:43-48	10:13-16
6:9-15	12:28-34
6:19-21	
7:1-5	Luke 7:36-50
9:3-13	15:1-32
11:16-19	17:11-21
13:44-46	
18:21-35	
20:1-15	

- Reflect on the FOCUS statement and the REVIEW OF CONTENTS questions.

FOCUS

The reign of God, the heart of the preaching and ministry of Jesus, has no one definition. It is God's saving presence revealed in Jesus' healings and exorcisms and in Jesus' sayings and parables. In the sayings, the parables, the Lord's Prayer, the use of wisdom sayings, Jesus indicates that the reign of God is now but is not yet. Jesus' preaching of the reign of God presumes that the disciples will begin to live in a new way and that the experience of redemption and reconciliation will become a reality in their lives.

OPENING PRAYER

Leader:
Jesus preached and so made present in his world the saving presence of God. The reign of God is this saving presence and action of God on our behalf. Let us respond to this good news by praying Psalm 85 (verses 8-14):

Right side:
Show us, O Lord, your kindness,
And grant us your salvation.

Left side:
I will hear what God proclaims.
Our God proclaims peace:
Peace to God's people, the faithful ones!
Peace to those who put their hope in God!

Right side:
Near indeed is God's salvation to us who love God,
Glory, dwelling in our midst.

Left side:
Kindness and truth shall meet, justice and peace shall kiss.
Truth shall spring out of the earth
and justice look down from heaven.

Right side:
The Lord will give us blessings.
Justice shall walk before our God
and salvation along the way of God's steps.

Leader:
This word of God does what it says: kindness, truth, justice, peace meet in our hearts, and in our group. Let us pause, and pray that such good news might sink in and bear fruit. We ask this in Jesus' name.

All:
Amen.

Song

REVIEW OF CONTENTS

What characteristic of the reign of God is most evident in each of these sayings and stories?

1. Luke 17:11-21

2. Mark 10:13-16

3. Luke 15:8-10

4. Matthew 6:19-21

5. Mark 4:26-29

VIDEO

The Reign of God and the Parables of Jesus

As you view this video, make note of the following:

What characteristics of the reign of God are revealed in these parables?

a. The Yeast _____

_____

b. The Great Feast _____

_____

c. The Laborers in the Field _____

_____

2. What are the qualities of a disciple described in these parables?

a. The Rich Man and Lazarus _____

_____

b. The Good Samaritan _____

_____

BREAK

(10 minutes)

LEARNING ACTIVITY

What quality of discipleship is found in each petition of the Lord's Prayer?

The Lord's Prayer	Characteristics of a Disciple
(Mt 6:9-13)	
Our Father, who art in heaven, hallowed be thy name;	
Thy kingdom come; thy will be done on earth as it is in heaven.	
Give us this day our daily bread;	
and forgive us our debts as we also have forgiven our debtors;	
And lead us not into temptation, but deliver us from evil.	

FAITH SHARING

The Parable of the Unmerciful Servant

Narrator: Then Peter came up and asked him,

Peter: "Lord, when my brother wrongs me, how often, must I forgive him? Seven times?"

Jesus: "No, not seven times; I say, seventy times seven times."

Narrator: That is why the reign of God may be said to be like a king who decided to settle accounts with his officials. When he began his auditing, one was brought in who owed him a huge amount. As he had no way of paying it, his master ordered him to be sold, along with his wife, his children, and all his property in payment of the debt. At that the official prostrated himself in homage and said,

Official: "My lord, be patient with me and I will pay you back in full."

Narrator: Moved with pity the master let the official go and wrote off the debt. But when that same official went out he met a fellow servant who owed him a mere fraction of what he himself owed. He seized him and throttled him.

Official: "Pay back what you owe."

Narrator: His fellow servant dropped to his knees and began to plead with him,

Servant: "Just give me time, and I will pay you back in full!"

Narrator: But he would hear none of it. Instead he had him put in jail until he paid back what he owed. When his fellow servants saw what had happened they were badly shaken, and went to their master to report the whole incident. His master sent for him and said:

King: "I cancelled your entire debt when you pleaded with me. Should you not have dealt mercifully with your fellow servant, as I dealt with you?"

Narrator: Then in anger the master handed him over to the torturers until he paid back all that he owed.

Jesus: "My heavenly Father will treat you in exactly the same way unless each of you forgives your brother (or sister) from your heart."

Reflection Questions

1. What connection do you see between this parable and the Lord's Prayer?

2. Why do you think the unmerciful servant failed to grant his fellow servant's request?

3. Why would Jesus tell a story of forgiveness in which the person forgiven was not changed by the experience?

4. Is there any relationship in your life that this parable addresses?

CLOSING PRAYER

A Call to Remember

Leader:
The reign of God "is God's saving presence revealed in Jesus' healings and exorcisms and in Jesus' sayings and parables . . . an experience of redemption and reconciliation." God's saving presence is made visible and tangible in Jesus' own self.

Reader:
A reading from the gospel according to Mark (4:26-29).

All:
Glory to you, O Lord.

A Call to Grow

The leader gives each participant a seed, saying: May the word of Christ grow in your mind and heart. Each responds: Amen!

Leader:
Let us pray together, in the words of Matthew, the Our Father . . .

Leader:
Let us go in peace to love and serve the Lord and be signs of God's reign in our world.

All:
Thanks be to God!

Concluding Song

REMINDER FOR NEXT WEEK:
We will use your own versions of the Lord's Prayer to be written in the follow-up journal exercise in our opening prayer next week.

FOLLOW-UP

A. Journaling

Rewrite the Lord's Prayer in your own words.

Or, reread the parable of the unmerciful servant in terms of your own life.

- Have you been forgiven and yet refused to give forgiveness?

- Have you ever made unrealistic demands on another? What are reasons why you have withheld forgiveness?

- What does the parable say to your life?

- Or perhaps you have tried to reconcile and your attempt has been rejected? Does the parable say anything to that situation?

Or, what contemporary situations calling for forgiveness and reconciliation come to mind in reading one of the parables? Write a parable for today. How does the message of the parable apply to this current situation? Is there a way in which your study group could help this situation?

B. Additional Resources

1. Read: Anthony Marinelli, *Understanding the Gospels,* Chapter 3, "The Coming of the Reign of God," pp. 33-53.

2. Read: Raymond E. Brown, S.S., *Responses to 101 Questions on the Bible,* Questions 45-51.

4. The Resurrection of Jesus

Preparation

- Read Perkins, Chapter 5, "The Resurrection of Jesus."
- Read the accounts of the resurrection appearances in Mark 16:1-20; Matthew 28:1-20; Luke 24; John 20.
- Reflect on the FOCUS statement and the REVIEW OF CONTENTS Questions.

FOCUS

In the accounts of the empty tomb and the post-resurrection appearance narratives, there are two key aspects: the empty tomb and the disciples' experience of the risen Christ. The discovery of the empty tomb left the disciples "half joyful, half fearful," and unable to comprehend what had happened. The Easter appearances of Jesus are the primary way in which the disciples came to know that Jesus was raised. Mary Magdalene, Mary, the mother of James, the other Mary, Peter and all the other disciples have seen for themselves and have come to believe. Through their testimony, we believe. The disciples interpreted the events that they experienced in the light of the Scriptures. This experience of the resurrection, in turn, gave new meaning to the Scriptures.

This session will focus on the background to the resurrection and explore those aspects which made it difficult for the disciples to grasp the reality of resurrection. We will look at the narratives of the empty tomb to discern their importance in building up resurrection faith and see what it is the gospels tell us about the risen Christ in the appearance stories.

OPENING PRAYER

Gathering Prayer

Leader:
Let us pray . . .

All:
Amen!

Leader:
Those who are prepared, please pray your own version of the Lord's Prayer now, leaving some moments of reflection after each one prays.

Song

Emmaus, located several miles from Jerusalem.

REVIEW OF CONTENTS

1. Read one of the accounts of the empty tomb narratives: Mark 16:1-8; Matthew 28:1-20; Mark 16:9-20; Luke 24; John 20. Use these questions to guide your reading:

When did the story take place?

Who were the women involved?

Why did the women come to the tomb?

What was seen?

What was said?

How did the women react?

2. What are the assertions that are made in the gospel passages?

3. Do the gospel accounts make the empty tomb a proof of the resurrection? Why or why not?

VIDEO

Interpreting the Resurrection

As you view this video, make note of the following:

1. What was meant by the suffering of the righteous?

_____

2. What did the Pharisees believe about the resurrection on the last day?

_____

What did the Sadducees believe?

_____

With which group did Jesus agree on this question?

_____

3. How did the appearance of the risen Jesus affect his disciples?

_____

_____

BREAK

(10 minutes)

LEARNING ACTIVITY

Reflect again on the passage you read in the Review of Contents section (Mark 16:1-8; Matthew 28:1-20; Mark 16:9-20; Luke 24; John 20).

What do you consider the fundamental message of the passage to be?

What images or ideas do you think of when you hear the word resurrection?

What images does this gospel passage use to convey the idea of resurrection?

Share what you have written with members of your small group.

FAITH SHARING

Read Luke 24:13-35, the appearance of Jesus on the Road to Emmaus. Think of one word that summarizes each one of these sections:

Luke 24:13-16

Luke 24:16-24

Luke 24:25-27

Luke 24:28-32

Luke 24:33-35

Share the word you chose with members of your group. Why did you choose that particular word?

As time allows, share your response to these questions in your small group.

1. Luke says that the disciples were "restrained from recognizing him." What do you think some of these restraints might have been?

2. What keeps you from recognizing Jesus "on the way"?

3. How did the disciples come to recognize him?

4. How were the disciples transformed by their awareness that Jesus was risen?

5. How are you transformed by your faith in the resurrection?

CLOSING PRAYER

Song

A Call to Remember

Reader:
A reading from St. Paul's first letter to the Corinthians
(from 1 Cor 15:4-10). . .

This is the word of the Lord.

All:
Thanks be to God!

Litany

Reader:
We recognized him in the breaking of the bread (Lk
24:35).

All:
All I want is to know him and the power flowing from
his resurrection (Phil 3:10).

Reader:
This is eternal life, risen life right now: to know you, the
one true God and the one whom you sent, Jesus Christ
(Jn 17:3).

All:
All I want is to know him and the power flowing from
his resurrection.

Reader:
He is the wisdom of God and the power of God (1 Cor
1:24).

All:

All I want is to know him and the power flowing from his resurrection.

Reader:

Our Father and Mother who art in heaven, hallowed be thy name.

All:

All I want is to know him and the power flowing from his resurrection.

Reader:

Give us this day our daily bread.

All:

All I want is to know him and the power flowing from his resurrection.

Reader:

And lead us not into temptation, but deliver us from evil, for the kingdom, the power and the glory are yours, now and forever. Amen.

All:

All I want is to know him and the power flowing from his resurrection.

Leader:

Let us go in peace to love and serve the risen Lord, Jesus!

All:
Thanks be to God!

Concluding Song

The Church of the Holy Sepulchre is built over the traditional sites of Golgotha and Jesus' tomb.

FOLLOW-UP

A. Journaling

In the conclusion of John's gospel it says that "Jesus performed many other signs—signs not recorded here—in the presence of his disciples. But these have been recorded to help you believe that Jesus is the Messiah, the Son of God, so that through this faith you might have life in his name" (Jn 20:30-31).

List as many words as you can which are images of the resurrection to you.

List as many words as you can that are images of death to you.

How many of these words are connected with events in your life?

How many of these words are connected with people in your life?

What relationships, events, people are life giving for you?

When have you experienced a death that has led to new life?

How has faith given you "life in his name"?

When Thomas saw the risen Lord he said, "My Lord and my God!" During the Eucharist we proclaim, "Christ has died, Christ is risen, Christ will come again!" Write your own personal affirmation of faith in the risen Lord.

B. Additional Resources

1. Read: Anthony Marinelli, *Understanding the Gospels,* Chapter 6, "The Death and Resurrection of Jesus," pp. 94-109.

2. Read: Raymond E. Brown, S.S., *Responses to 101 Questions on the Bible,* Questions 52-53.

3. Read: *The Catholic Study Bible,* commentary on the resurrection narratives, RG 404, 416, 435, 448.

4. Using the Hammond *Atlas of the Bible Lands,* find the places referred to in these passages: Mark 16:7; Matthew 28:10; Luke 24:13,33,50; John 21:1.

5. The Beginnings of Christology

Preparation

- Read Perkins, Chapter 6, "The Beginnings of Christology."
- Read the following New Testament texts: Philippians 2:6-11, 1 Corinthians 8:6, 1 Corinthians 15:15-20, John 1:1-18.
- Reflect on the FOCUS statement and the REVIEW OF CONTENTS questions.

FOCUS

What we find in the New Testament is an expression of faith. The first Christians experienced the love, mercy and forgiveness of God when they encountered Jesus. The New Testament is about their struggle to put that experience into words. Before they wrote about it, or even told a comprehensive story, they first celebrated their experience in prayer and worship. Stories about Jesus were handed on in the context of the liturgy. They also attributed titles to Jesus. Some of these were Messiah, Son of Man, and Lord. Such titles carried a rich meaning from the Old Testament. The first Christians used these titles to name who Jesus was from their experience. This was the beginning of what theologians today call christology: the study of the identity and role of Jesus.

OPENING PRAYER

Opening Song

Leader:
Let us pray . . .

Psalm 89

Right side:
Happy are we who walk in the light of your face O Lord,
for kindness and truth go before you.
At your name we rejoice all the day,
for you have given us our King.

Left side:
Once you spoke to us, and to your faithful ones you said:
On a champion I have placed my crown;
I have found my servant and anointed him with holy oil.
My hand is always with him, my arm makes him strong.
My faithfulness and kindness shall be with him.

Right side:
He shall say of me:
"You are my father, my God, the rock, my savior."
I will make him first born, highest of the kings of the
    earth.

Left side:
Forever I will maintain my kindness toward him,
and my covenant with him stands firm.

Concluding Song

REVIEW OF CONTENTS

1. What is christology? How does the christology of to-day's theologians differ from that of New Testament authors? (See Perkins, pp. 110 and 112.)

2. The christology that we find in the New Testament is greatly affected by the early Christians' experience of the resurrection of Jesus. (See Perkins, pp. 100-101, and the biblical texts to which she refers.)

a. What divine functions are attributed to the exalted Jesus?

b. How is the role of the exalted Jesus seen to be like that of the angels in Daniel 7:14-15?

c. How is Jesus' role seen to differ from that of the angels? (Check Hebrews 1 which contains Old Testament references supporting the idea that Jesus is "far superior to" and possesses a relationship with God beyond that of any of the angels.)

3. In attempting to express who they understood Jesus to be the first Christians used titles that were available to them mainly from the Jewish Scriptures.

a. What were some of the associated meanings of the following titles that were applied to Jesus? (Summarized by Perkins, pp. 101-106.)

i. Messiah (or Christ) (see also 2 Sam 23:1-17).

ii. Son of Man (see also Dan 7).

iii. Son of God (see also Ps 2:7).

iv. Lord.

b. Why did the suffering and death of Jesus present a problem in understanding Jesus as Messiah? (Perkins, p. 102)

c. How did the Jewish Christians deal with the problem of distinguishing Jesus (as Lord) from God (as Lord)? Why did the early Christians rarely speak of Jesus as God? (See pages 106 and 109 of Perkins.)

4. What do scholars believe is the origin of the hymns, such as Phil 2:6-11, that are incorporated into the New Testament? (Perkins discusses this on p. 107.)

VIDEO

New Testament Christologies

As you view this video, please make note of the following:

1. What is christology? _____

_____

2. What do the following titles of Jesus mean in the New Testament? Note that these meanings are not necessarily the same as those they have acquired in the subsequent evolution of the Church's faith.

a. Christ _____

b. Lord _____

c. Son of God_____

BREAK

(10 minutes)

LEARNING ACTIVITY

Group A

Read carefully Philippians 2:6-11. (Perkins quotes this passage on 107-108.) Then discuss the following questions. Record your answers. Using the textbook to read this passage leaves Bibles free for locating the other passages more conveniently.

1. At the beginning of this hymn, there is a hint of Jesus' special relationship to God: "He was in the form of God." Check 1 Corinthians 8:6. How is Jesus described in this passage?

Compare this description of Jesus to the role of the "wisdom" of God in Wisdom 9:9 and Proverbs 3:19.

2. Read the references to Adam and Eve in Genesis 2:15-17 and 3:22-24. How is Jesus contrasted with Adam and Eve in the hymn in Philippians 2?

3. Summarize the following references to Jesus and obedience in the gospels:
a. Matthew 26:39, 42
b. John 4:34, 5:30, 6:38
c. Mark 3:35
d. Matthew 7:21

4. Jesus was without sin (see 2 Cor 5:21). Therefore, his death could not be seen as a punishment for sin. However, crucifixion was a scandal in first century Judaism. Only the worst criminals suffered crucifixion. According to this hymn, how did the first Christians come to understand and explain Jesus' death?

5. Read Isaiah 52:13-15 and 53:12. How does this help us to understand the meaning of the phrases, "humbling himself" and "being exalted" in the Philippians hymn?

6. Use your own words to compose a brief (five or six sentences) summary of what the first Christians were saying about Jesus in this hymn. Someone should be prepared to read this summary to the large group.

Group B

Read carefully Colossians 1:15-20. Discuss and record your answers to the following questions:

1. How is Jesus the "image of the invisible God"? See John 1:18.

2. Jesus is described as the "first-born" of God. What do the following Old Testament references say about God's first-born? To whom does each passage refer?
a. Psalm 89:27-28
b. Exodus 4:22-23
c. Proverbs 8:22-31

How does Christ's place as "first-born" differ from those described in the first two passages above?

How does Christ's role compare to the Wisdom of God as "first-born" described in Proverbs 8?

3. a. What is Jesus' relationship to the angels (thrones, dominations, principalities, and powers), according to this hymn?

b. What does Ephesians 1:20-21 say about Jesus' relationship to the angels?

4. a. How are the Church and Jesus related? (Read also Rom 12:3-8).

b. What does this relationship imply about how Jesus will continue to be in the world?

5. Jesus is also a reconciler through his death on the cross, according to this hymn. Read Ephesians 2:11-21. Describe the example of "reconciliation in Christ" that is given here.

6. Compose a brief (five or six sentences) summary of what the first Christians who prayed or sang this hymn were expressing about who Jesus was. Someone should be prepared to read the summary to the larger group.

FAITH SHARING

1. Make a list of the titles of Jesus that have most meaning for you, or that you commonly use in addressing Jesus. These do not have to be biblical titles.

2. Is there a prayer or hymn (liturgical or personal) that best expresses who Jesus is for you? Make a note of it.

3. Why do these titles, prayers, and/or hymns appeal to you? What aspects of your understanding of Jesus do they express?

You will be invited to share your reflections with the group.

CLOSING PRAYER

Song

A Call to Remember

Reader:
A reading from the book of Exodus (34:6) . . .
This is the word of the Lord.

All:
Thanks be to God!

A Call to Respond

Leader:
Let us respond to this good news with this New Testament hymn from John's gospel which celebrates the *hesed* and *'emit* of God, translated here as the grace and truth of God, taking our human flesh.

Right side:
He came to his own . . . and to those who did accept him he gave the power to become the children of God.

Left side:
The Word became flesh and dwelt among us.

Right side:
We have seen his glory, the glory of the Father's only Son, full of grace and truth, full of *hesed* and *'emit*.

Left side:
Out of his fullness we have all received grace upon grace upon grace upon grace.

Right side:
The law was given through Moses, but grace and truth, *hesed* and *'emit,* have come through Jesus Christ.

Left Side:
No one has ever seen God, but the one who is closest to the Father's heart has made God known.

Leader:
Now let us join Jesus in his prayer.

All:
Our Father and Mother, who art in heaven . . .
for the kingdom, the power and the glory are yours now and forever.

Leader:
Let the glory and power be yours, our God. Let the glory you take in us flow from our being fully human, ever more and more alive to all that is of the earth. We thank you for Jesus, for his kindness and fidelity, for his obedience and humility, and especially for his being human, like us in all things. We pray in his name and in the power of the Holy Spirit.

All:
Amen.

Leader:
Let us now go to love and serve the Lord and glorify God in all that we do.

All:
Thanks be to God!

Concluding Song

REMINDER FOR NEXT WEEK:
You are invited to share something of your own image of Christ from your journal next session. Consider making up your own christological hymn, to paint, draw, compose music, or select art or music that speaks to you. We will begin out next session with this sharing.

FOLLOW-UP

A. Journaling

Think about how you have experienced Jesus in your life. Which roles of Jesus seem to have most meaning for you? Does the exaltation of Jesus, his presence from the beginning of creation, his headship of the church, for example, have any meaning for you? Do you have favorite artistic representations of Jesus (pictures, statues)? Which aspects of Jesus' life, death and resurrection are expressed in those?

Write your own christological hymn or prayer on the basis of these reflections. (You may want to represent your ideas in drawing, painting or music.)

B. Additional Resources

1. Here are some other prayers and hymns found in the New Testament to read and reflect on:

    Luke 1:46-55 (The Magnificat)
    Luke 1:68-79 (The Benedictus)
    Luke 2:29-32
    Colossians 1:15-20
    Ephesians 1:3-10
    1 Peter 1:3-9
    Acts 4:23-31 (community prayer)

2. Read: Anthony Marinelli, *Understanding the Gospels,* "Titles of Christ in the Synoptic Gospels," pp. 58-59.

3. Read: Raymond E. Brown, S.S., *Responses to 101 Questions on the Bible,* Questions 69-76.

4. Using the Hammond *Atlas of the Bible Lands,* locate the following places which are associated with the Scriptures studied in the session: Caeserea Philippi, Philippi, Corinth, Colossae, Ephesus.

6. Mark: Jesus, Suffering Messiah

Preparation

- Read Perkins, Chapter 12, "Mark: Jesus, Suffering Messiah."
- Read Mark 2:1-3:6 and 8:22-10:52.
- Reflect on the FOCUS statement and the REVIEW OF CONTENTS questions.

FOCUS

One of the major themes of Mark's gospel is that Jesus, the powerful savior, saves not by an assertion of divine or human power, but through his suffering. Likewise, his disciples will be called upon to suffer. Mark's gospel seems to be addressed to a suffering community. Peter has been martyred (ca. A.D. 64) and the community faces misunderstanding and rejection. There is an apparent need to deal with the relevance and meaning of this suffering in the light of the Christian mission.

OPENING PRAYER

Leader:
Grace and peace be with you.

All:
And also with you!

Leader:
We are assembled in small groups so that we might share personally some of what Christ means to us. Our listening and receiving each other without judging is a kind of contemplation. To empty our heads and hearts of the many voices we bring here and in order to be more open to receive, let us now close our eyes and breathe deeply . . .

Song

REVIEW OF CONTENTS

Recall and briefly write in the spaces provided your response to each of the following questions. References to Perkins and to the gospel of Mark are provided where appropriate for easy review. Be prepared to share your responses with the group and to support them when called upon by your program leader.

1. Make a list of five or six words or phrases that indicate what you understood the word ''gospel'' to mean prior to the reading for this session (or to this course).

2. What seems to be the original meaning of the word "gospel" as used by New Testament writers? (St. Paul's use—Perkins, p. 203).

3. What meaning does Mark give the word "gospel," in each of the following passages:
a. Mark 1:14-15
b. Mark 8:35, 10:29, 13:10, 14:9
c. Mark 14:9
What does Perkins suggest is the meaning of this last passage?

4. How does Mark's use of the word "gospel" compare to your understanding of the word expressed in number 1, above?

5. What does Perkins say is the theme of Mark's gospel? What events make up the center of the plot (p. 205)?

6. What is meant by the "messianic secret" in Mark? To what paradox does it point? (See Perkins, p. 205, Mk 1:40-45, 8:27-30, 9:9.)

VIDEO

The Cross in the Gospel of Mark

As you view this video, please make note of the following:

1. What were some of the special concerns facing Mark's audience?

_____

_____

2. Why does Peter argue with Jesus?

_____

_____

3. How do the other apostles respond to Jesus' message of the cross?

_____

_____

BREAK

(10 minutes)

LEARNING ACTIVITY

Divide into three (or more) groups as directed by your leader. Briefly make notes in the spaces provided as you research and discuss the questions related to one of the following passages (or set of passages) from Mark's gospel. Each group will be asked to contribute to an outline portrait of discipleship as presented by Mark (your responses to question 3) at the end of the activity.

View from Mt. Tabor looking north. Tabor is the traditional site of the Transfiguration.

Group 1

Read Mark 4.

1. Are there any clues here as to what Jesus' disciples were like? (Check verses 13 and 40-41, for example.)

2. What images are used to describe the reign of God (see vs. 26-29 and 30-32)? Explain what these images tell us about what the reign of God is like.

3. Make a list of the characteristics of a true disciple as these are revealed in the chapter of Mark. Note the verses that support your answer.

Characteristic of discipleship   **Supporting verses**

Group 2

Read Mark 10:13-45.

1. What words and phrases are used in this passage to describe the attitudes and behaviors of Jesus' followers? (Check verses 13, 24-26, 32, and 35-37.) Do you think they were really aware of the true nature of Jesus' mission and of the reign of God? Explain.

2. With what words of Jesus does Mark express what is expected of a true disciple? Are there any words of encouragement or hope? If so, what are they?

3. List the characteristics of the true disciple that are revealed in this passage. Support your answers by noting the verses to which you are referring.

Characteristic of discipleship   **Supporting verses**

Group 3

Read Mark 1:14-20, 2:13-17, 13:9-13.

1. Summarize briefly the words and actions of Jesus and his disciples that show the urgency of becoming a disciple. (Check 1:14-15; 1:18; and 13:9). What impressions are given about the kind of kingdom Jesus has come to establish?

2. What does Jesus require of his disciples, those who will be members of his kingdom?

3. Make a list of the characteristics of discipleship revealed in these gospel passages. Note the verses which support your answers.

Characteristic of discipleship   **Supporting verses**

All groups

As your leader collects the lists of characteristics of discipleship compiled by all the groups, copy the compilation below for future reference.

FAITH SHARING

1. Reflect on the characteristics of a disciple as presented in Mark's gospel. Which of these characteristics do you think are especially valuable for Christians today? Choose one or two and explain your choice.

2. Which characteristics do you think are the most difficult to acquire in today's world? Why?

3. How can modern Christian disciples offer hope and support to one another? Is Mark's gospel helpful in this regard? Explain.

CLOSING PRAYER

A Call to Respond

Song

Reading

Reader:
A reading from the gospel according to Mark (10:17-18, 21).

All:
Glory to you, O Lord.

Litany

Leader:
Now we will look at him tenderly as we watch his suffering all through his life, suffering so very much like our own. Let us respond to these gospel sentences by praying: You are like us, Lord.

Reader:
When your solitude is spoiled (1:35-38),

All:
You are like us, Lord.

Reader:
When you are accused and harassed (2:7),

All:
You are like us, Lord.

. . . .

All:
You are like us, Lord.

Leader:
Let us pray.

All:
Lord Jesus, our brother and our friend, thank you for being like us in everything, for knowing in your very body how painful our limits and weakness really are. Thank you for sharing life with us. We ask for the deepening of your Spirit within us so that we may grow more and more like you in everything, day by day. Unite us with one another and with all your church, your body which still suffers throughout the world. Look on us all tenderly as we keep our eyes fixed on you. We ask and praise and thank in your name. Amen.

Leader:
We continue to pray in Jesus' name:

All:
Our Father and Mother . . .
for the kingdom, the power and the glory are yours, now and forever. Amen.

Leader:
Let us go to love and serve our Suffering Servant and one another.

All:
Thanks be to God.

Concluding Song

FOLLOW-UP

A. Journaling

In Mark's gospel, Jesus is almost always with his disciples. They are called at the outset of the gospel (Mk 1). Because of the inability of his disciples to understand, in most of what Jesus says and does, he is alone. They fall asleep while he suffers in Gethsemane and abandon him in his death. Even at the news of his resurrection, they flee in bewilderment and fear (Mk 16:8).

Read one or more of the following passages. In what incidents in your life do you identify with the solitary Jesus? When do you identify with the bewildered disciples? What are the sources of your strength in those times?

Mark 6:1-6—Jesus not accepted in his "own part of the country."

Mark 8:14-21—Disciples do not understand the multiplication of the loaves.

Mark 9:30-32—Disciples fail to understand the approaching death of Jesus.

Mark 14:32-42—Gethsemane.

Mark 14:43-52—Jesus is arrested.

Mark 14:66-72—Peter's denial of Jesus.

B. Additional Resources

1. Read over as much of Mark's gospel as time allows using the outline in Perkins, p. 206 as a guide.

2. If your Bible has an introduction to Mark's gospel, read it.

3. Read: Anthony Marinelli, *Understanding the Gospels,* Chapter 4, "The Synoptic Gospels," pp. 54-60.

4. Read: *The Catholic Study Bible,* "Mark," RG 405-417.

5. Scholars believe that Mark's audience was probably the Christian community in Rome. Using your Hammond *Atlas of the Bible Lands,* locate Rome.

7. Matthew: Jesus, Teacher of Israel

Preparation

- Read Perkins, Chapter 13, "Matthew: Jesus, Teacher of Israel."
- Read the sermons in Matthew:

Matthew 5:1-7:29	Matthew 18:1-35
Matthew 9:35-11:1	Matthew 19:1-20:34
Matthew 13:1-53	Matthew 24:1-25:46

- Reflect on the FOCUS statement and the REVIEW OF CONTENTS questions.

"The kingdom of heaven belongs to such as these" (Mt 19:14).

FOCUS

Matthew's community is believed to have been made up primarily of Jewish Christians. By the time of the composition of his gospel, however, the community that believed in Jesus found itself outside the confines of Judaism. This led to many conflicts, both external and internal. The early Jewish Christians faced opposition and rejection by their former Jewish communities, but neither were they Gentiles. Matthew tries to offer an interpretation of their situation that encompasses both continuity with their past and an incorporation of the newness in Jesus' mission and message. Within the community, disagreements and friction were also present. The reign of God did not seem to produce perfection. Should not the messiah have brought total peace and happiness? Many became discouraged; their faith grew cold. Matthew encourages his community to trust in the power of Jesus and his continued presence. He shows how the ambiguities will continue to exist while the reign of God is in this world, but at the end of time things will be different. Jesus' followers are to listen to Jesus' teaching, through which they will know how to be faithful disciples.

OPENING PRAYER

Song

O Come, O Come Emmanuel!

Psalms 124 and 91

Right side:
Had not the Lord been with us, let Israel say—
had not the Lord been with us—
when enemies rose up against us,
they would have swallowed us alive.

Left side:
The torrent would have swept over us,
over us would have swept the raging water.
Blessed be the Lord who did not leave us.

Right side:
We were set free like a bird from the hunter's trap.
The trap was broken and we were freed.

Left side:
To the angels God has given command about us,
that they guard us in all our ways.
On their hands they bear us up,
lest we dash our foot against a rock.

Right side:
Because you cling to me I will deliver you, says the Lord.
I will set you on high because you acknowledge my
    name.

Left side:
You will call upon me and I will answer you.
I will be with you in distress.
I will deliver and glorify you and will show you my sal-
    vation.

All:
(Repeat the opening song)
O Come, O Come Emmanuel . . .

REVIEW OF CONTENTS

In this exercise, you will be asked to compare some of
the introductory passages of Mark's gospel with their
parallels in Matthew, as suggested in Perkins, chapter 13.
The final question will help you review and summarize
the results of this comparison. Read the given passages
from the gospels and answer the questions as directed by
your leader.

1. Read both Mark's and Matthew's accounts of the ministry of John the Baptist (Mark 1:2-8 and Matthew 3:1-12).

a. Note the verses in Matthew's text that also occur in
Mark's text.

b. How does Matthew "correct" Mark 1:2? What concerns
of Matthew are reflected in this change? (See Perkins, p.
215.)

c. Read the content of John's preaching, verses 7-12 in
Matthew. Does Mark include these texts? Why do scholars
conclude that Matthew took these sayings from Q? (See
Perkins, p. 215, par. 2.)

Which theme of Matthew is being emphasized in the
preaching of Jesus here?

What is the reason for Matthew's emphasis on this theme? (See Perkins, p. 215.)

d. Luke 3:7 says, "He would say to the crowds that came out to be baptized by him: 'You brood of vipers!'" To whom does Matthew's gospel address the same condemnation (Mt 3:7)?

According to Perkins, what seems to be the explanation of this difference between Luke and Matthew (p. 215)?

2. Read carefully the parallel texts about the baptism of Jesus: Matthew 3:13-17 and Mark 1:9-11.

a. Note the text in Matthew that is also found in Mark.

b. What are the two major changes that Matthew has made in this account of Jesus' baptism? (See Perkins, p. 215.)

c. Why do you think Matthew wants to show that Jesus fulfills God's plan (vs. 14)?

3. Read and compare the accounts of Jesus' testing in the wilderness in Mark 1:12-13 and Matthew 4:1-11.

a. Notice that very little of this Matthew text occurs in the account by Mark. Most of Matthew's account, however, can be found in Luke's gospel. What does this indicate about the source of the content of the temptations of Jesus? (See Perkins, p. 216.)

b. Both the tempter and Jesus use citations from the Old Testament (Deuteronomy and Psalms). Since this incident occurs at the beginning of Jesus' public life, what does it reveal about how we might expect Jesus to relate to the Old Law? (See footnote to Mt 4:1-11 in NAB; also Perkins, p. 221.)

4. Read and compare the following accounts of the initiation of Jesus' preaching of the kingdom of God: Mark 1:14-15 and Matthew 4:12-17.

a. Note the presence of Mark's material in Matthew's version of the beginning of Jesus' preaching. What phrases within this material, especially in the "words of Jesus" differ between the two accounts? Suggest explanations of these differences (Perkins, p. 216).

b. What does Perkins suggest is the significance of the increased geographic region that Jesus covers and addresses here and in other parts of his gospel? (See Perkins pp. 216

and 218; the footnote to Mt 4:12-17 in NAB is also helpful.)

5. Summary discussion questions:

a. Mark's gospel is the obvious source of some of Matthew's text, as you saw from the comparisons above.
What were the other sources corresponding to the following material in Matthew:

- the material found in both Matthew and Luke,
  for example the content of Jesus' testing in the
  wilderness?

- prophetic sayings, such as Mt 4:15-16?

- texts, such as those condemning the Pharisees
  (Mt 3:7), found only in Matthew?

b. What concerns or themes of Matthew and his community
have you identified from the passages above? The answer
to this question should be an accumulation of answers from
the four questions above.

VIDEO

Matthew: The Wise Scribe

As you view this video, please make note of the following:

1. What was the position of each of these persons or groups concerning the place of the Gentiles within the Church?

Judaizers _____

Paul _____

Peter and James _____

2. What was Matthew's main concern in writing his gospel?

_____

BREAK

(10 minutes)

LEARNING ACTIVITY

In this activity, you will be asked by your leader to study and discuss one of the five sermons of Jesus presented in Matthew's gospel. This will be done in a group, according to your leader's directions. Questions are provided to aid your investigation of each sermon. At the end of the activity, your group will be asked to share with all the participants some of the reflections on the questions you have discussed. Make notes in the space provided to aid your memory and discussion.

Group 1

The Sermon on the Mount, Matthew 5:1-7:29.

1. How do you picture this sermon taking place? (Describe the setting, vs. 1-2.)

2. Summarize Jesus' sayings about the following issues in this sermon:

a. relationship of Christ and his kingdom to the Old Law (5:17-19)

b. rifts between members of the community (5:22, 23-25; 7:1-5; 7:12)

c. relationship to outsiders (5:43-48)

3. How are Jesus' followers to distinguish between a true prophet and a false one, a true disciple and a false one (7:15-23)?

4. Matthew 7:24-27 contrasts two types of foundations on which Jesus' followers can build their lives. To what does he compare these foundations? Using the information you gathered in questions 1-3 above, summarize briefly what this sermon presents as a firm foundation for the true disciple of Jesus.

Group 2

The Disciple on Mission to Israel, Matthew 9:35-11:1.

1. What kind of person does Matthew show Jesus to be at the beginning of this sermon (9:35-38)? To whom is the sermon addressed (10:1-4)? To whom are the apostles being sent (10:5-6)?

2. In your own words, describe the message and ministry the apostles are to bring to the people, as presented in the following texts:
a. 10:7-8
b. 10:27
c. 10:37-39

3. How are the apostles to conduct themselves? (Check 10:9-10, 10:11-14, 10:17-20.)

What practical concern lies behind the promise of a reward for those who welcome Jesus' disciples, as in 10:40-42? (See Perkins, p. 220.)

4. Jesus speaks words of encouragement to his apostles. Summarize the sources of hope Jesus offers to those who undertake this mission in his name. (See especially the following verses in chapter 10:15, 20, 30-33, 38-39, 40-42.)

Group 3

The Parables of the Kingdom, Matthew 13:1-53.

1. Describe the setting the location and audience for this sermon of Jesus (13:1-2).

2. Recall that in Mark's gospel the disciples of Jesus generally responded in fear and misunderstanding to the teachings of Jesus. How do the disciples in Matthew's gospel compare? (Check 13:11, 16, 51.)

3. What does Jesus ask of his disciples in Matthew's presentation of the parables of the treasure and the pearl (vs. 44-46)?

What do the parables of the mustard seed and the leaven (vs. 31-33) tell us about how the reign of God grows in this world?

4. According to Jesus' parables presented in this sermon, what is the difference between the reign of God as it exists in this world now and the final reign of God as it will exist at the end of the world? (Check vs. 29-30, 37-43, 47-50.)

Why might this teaching of Jesus about the distinction between the kingdom now and the kingdom yet to come be significant and helpful to Matthew's community?

Group 4

Relationships within the Community, Matthew 18:1-35.

1. What prompts Jesus to give this sermon? How does the sermon begin? To whom is it addressed (vs. 1, 21)?

2. What does Jesus' reference to children in this sermon (vs. 12-14) tell us about what it means to be a disciple? (See Perkins, p. 225.)

3. What kind of problems within this early Christian community does Matthew seem to address in the following verses of this sermon:

a. 6-7
b. 15-16
c. 21-35

4. Recall that Jesus is addressing his disciples, the leaders of the community here. Peter, for example, is present (vs. 21). What message is Jesus giving them in vs. 12-14?

5. Matthew also offers words of comfort and hope to his community in this sermon of Jesus. Summarize this message presented in verses 18 and 19-20.

Group 5

The End of the World and Judgment, Matthew 24:1-25:46.

1. To whom is Jesus speaking in this sermon? Where is he and when does it take place (24:1-4, 26:1-2)?

2. Matthew's community is confused by the continued presence of evil after the reign of God has already been initiated by Jesus. Briefly state how this problem is addressed in the following verses from this text.

a. 24:11-14
b. 24:30-35
c. 24:44-51
d. 25:1-13

3. In chapter 25, those who will be saved are contrasted with those who will not through three sets of images. What does each of the following sets of images tell us about what it means to be a true disciple of Jesus:

a. wise virgins and foolish virgins

b. servants who invested their silver pieces and servants who buried their silver pieces

c. the sheep and the goats

FAITH SHARING

1. Reflect back on your own reading and research in Matthew's gospel as well as that learned from the video presentation. Are the concerns of Matthew and his community very similar, somewhat similar, or totally different from those you experience in your present Christian community? Explain.

2. Are Matthew's words of warning regarding how we are to be judged relevant to Christians today? Why or why not?

3. Which words of comfort and hope in Matthew's gospel did you find especially helpful to your situation in Christian community today (your family, friends, parish)? How so?

CLOSING PRAYER

A Call to Remember

Reader:
A reading from the gospel according to Matthew (9:9-13):

All:
Glory to you, O Lord.

Reader:
This is the gospel of the Lord.

All:
Praise to you, Lord Jesus Christ!

A Call to Respond

Leader:
"I desire mercy, not sacrifice," must have been important
to Matthew and his community, perhaps flowing from his
personal experience of having been so accepted and wel-
comed by the merciful Jesus. What gospel words are particularly important to you, words which you apply to
your life, your family, parish, world? What is good news
for you? Please share those words of good news with the
person next to you.

Leader:
Let us pray:
Let us stand, and in the Jewish manner of prayer, lift our
hands to God in supplication as we pray:

All:
Our Father and Mother who art in heaven . . .
for the kingdom, the power and the glory are yours, now
and forever. Amen.

Concluding Song
O Come, O Come, Emmanuel!

FOLLOW-UP

A. Journaling

Matthew presents Jesus as a great teacher. Jesus' words to his disciples and followers are very important in guiding their lives. His words reveal the will of God and the true meaning of God's law. Recall sayings of Jesus that are either particularly appealing to you, helpful in your life, or disturbing to you. You may want to leaf through Matthew's gospel to refresh your memory or discover sayings you were not aware of. Make a list of several sayings for each category. You may also wish to add other categories. Reflect on and write about the significance of one or two of these sayings in your life.

B. Additional Resources

1. Read as much as possible of the gospel of Matthew using the outline of the gospel in Perkins, p. 219.

2. If your Bible has an introduction to the gospel of Matthew, read it.

3. Read: Anthony Marinelli, *Understanding the Gospels,* Chapter 4, "The Synoptic Gospels," pp. 60-67.

4. Read: *The Catholic Study Bible,* "Matthew," RG 388-405.

5. Scholars believe that Matthew's community was in Antioch in Syria. Using the Hammond *Atlas of the Bible Lands,* locate Antioch.

8. Luke: Jesus the Lord

Preparation

- Read Perkins, Chapter 14, "Luke: Jesus the Lord."
- Read Luke 9:51-19:27.
- Reflect on the FOCUS statement and the REVIEW OF CONTENTS questions.

FOCUS

In the Gospel of Luke the ministry of Jesus is divided into three sections: his ministry in Galilee; his journey to Jerusalem; and his ministry in Jerusalem. Luke's journey narrative has three sections: 9:51-13:21; 13:22-17:10; and 17:11-19:27. The opening verse of each of these divisions states that Jesus was on his way to Jerusalem. "On the way" there are those who will accept Jesus and there are those who will reject him. Luke understands discipleship as a call to follow Jesus and the true disciple is the one who hears the word of God and keeps it (8:19-21). Luke's model of the "first disciple" is Mary, an example of faithfulness and wholehearted response to God's initiative. The disciples must leave all things to follow Jesus and to walk along the way that Jesus has set out for them.

OPENING PRAYER

Reader:
A reading from the prophet Isaiah (58:6-11) . . .

Reader:
This is the word of the Lord.

All:
Thanks be to God.

Psalm 146

Right side:
Bless the Lord, my whole life!
I will praise the Lord all my life;
I will sing praise to my God while I live.

Left side:
Happy are we whose help is God,
whose hope is in the Lord,

Model of the Temple in Jerusalem as it was at the time of Jesus.

our God who is faithful forever,
securing justice for the oppressed,
giving food to the hungry.

Right side:
The Lord sets captives free,
the Lord gives sight to the blind.
The Lord raises up those who were bent over.

Left side:
The Lord protects strangers;
the orphans and the widows God sustains,
but the way of the wicked God thwarts.

All:
Our God shall reign forever,
our Lord for all generations. Alleluia!

Reader:
A reading from the holy gospel according to Luke
(4:14-21).

All:
Glory to you, O Lord.

Reader:
This is the good news of the Lord.

All:
Praise to you, Lord Jesus Christ.

Leader:
Let us pray.

All:
Let your light, Lord Jesus, break forth in us like a dawn,
heal our wounds and open our eyes so that we may
know you and the power of your Spirit. We ask this in
your name. Amen.

REVIEW OF CONTENTS

Check the phrase(s) that most adequately completes the sentence:

1. According to the preface (vs.1-4), the main purpose of Luke's Gospel is:
>   to instruct Theophilus about the practical implications of being a Christian;
>   to write a history of Jesus and the first disciples;
>   to assure his readers that what the church preaches goes back to the preaching of Jesus and the earliest disciples.

2. The gospel of Luke incorporates much of the material that is found in Mark, and:
>   adds passages from Q;
>   includes sections that are unique to Luke;
>   uses the imagery from John's gospel.

3. Three major additions that Luke makes to Mark's gospel are: 1. most of the instructions given to the church on the journey to Jerusalem (9:51-19:27); 2. accounts of the resurrection appearances (24); and 3:
>   the call of the twelve apostles (6:12-16);
>   the account of Jesus' birth and early life (1:5-2:40);
>   the story of the temptation in the desert (4:1-13).

4. Luke divides the ministry of Jesus into 1. his Galilean ministry; 2. journey to Jerusalem; and 3. his ministry in Jerusalem. One of the common themes that binds these episodes together is:
>   the contrast of those who accept Jesus with those who reject him;
>   blocks of teaching organized into identifiable sermons;
>   the image of journey.

5. Jesus tells the parables of the lost sheep, the woman searching for a lost coin and the prodigal son (15:1-32) in order to:

teach that one must have care and concern for
   others;
give examples of God's love and mercy;
say that Christians ought to celebrate and rejoice.

6. The parables of the lost sheep, coin and prodigal son
focus on the basic issue between Jesus and the Lukan
Pharisees:
   No one is outside the circle of God's love;
   Salvation is offered even to the sinners and outcasts
      of society;
   Being religious involves more than the keeping of
      laws and regulations.

7. Jesus' opening sermon in Luke (4:16-30) proclaims that
the Scripture's promise of a time of salvation is fulfilled in
Jesus. Some signs of a new age of salvation are:
   repentance and celebrations of joy which are
      responses to Jesus' preaching;
   persons who praise and glorify God like Mary and
      Zechariah who bless God;
   the fall of the Roman empire.

8. In the threefold division of the gospel, Luke presents a
pattern of salvation history. The first period is God's
promises to Israel which includes those who wait for the
coming of the Lord like Simeon and Anna and culminates
in John the Baptist. The second period is Jesus' ministry.
The third period is:
   Jesus' death and resurrection;
   the second coming of Christ;
   the church's mission.

9. Luke presents Jesus as the universal savior. This univer-
salism manifests itself in the inclusion of non-Jews in
Christianity and in:
   the inclusion of the poor, the outcasts, women, and
      sinners;
   evangelizing the Emperor Augustus;
   letting the Samaritans pray in the synagogue.

VIDEO

Jesus' Journey to Jerusalem

As you view this video, please make note of the following:

1. What are the three stages of salvation history outlined by Luke?

a. _____

b. _____

c. _____

2. What are the qualities of a disciple which Luke outlines in his journey section?

a. _____

b. _____

c. _____

d. _____

e. _____

f. _____

BREAK

(10 minutes)

LEARNING ACTIVITY

Read the passage below which is assigned to you by your program leader. Make note of the character(s) who either accept or reject Jesus and how they are contrasted in the story.

Luke 2:25-38

Luke 4:16-30

Luke 7:36-50

Luke 9:51-54 and 17:11-19

Luke 23:39-43

In the passage you read, which characters or groups accept Jesus? Which reject him? How are they contrasted in the passage(s)?

What lesson is Luke teaching through these episodes of acceptance and rejection?

FAITH SHARING

Prayer was the primary way in which Jesus deepened his relationship with God. Throughout his gospel, Luke indicates how important prayer is in the life of Jesus. In every decisive moment of his life he is at prayer: after his baptism (3:21), at the beginning of his ministry (4:16), before choosing the twelve (6:12), in the synagogue (4:16), and on the mountain top (9:28). Luke gives examples of prayer in the Our Father (11:2-4) in the Canticles of Mary (1:46-55), Zechariah (68-79) and Simeon (2:29-32). The disciples are admonished to pray always (18:1) and are assured that their prayer will not go unheard (11:5-13).

Read Luke 18:1-8.

1. The widow is described as persistent and demanding of her rights under the law. Why is she so disturbing to the judge?

2. Why would Jesus use a corrupt judge as an example of the power of prayer?

3. What are some of the lessons of this parable for your own life?

4. Can you give any examples of times in which prayer has had power in your life?

CLOSING PRAYER

Luke's Prayers of Praise

Leader:
Let us pray.

"Blessed are you, God of Israel,
for you have visited and redeemed your people . . .
that we might serve you without fear,
in holiness and justice all the days of our lives."

"To give light to those who sit in darkness and the
    shadow of death,
To guide our feet in the way of peace."

Let us respond, using Mary's song.

All:
My heart proclaims your greatness, O my God,
And my spirit rejoices in you, my Savior!

Right side:
For you have looked on your servant tenderly.
You have blessed me, poor and a serving woman.

Left side:
From this day on, all generations will call me blessed.
For you, who are mighty, have done great things for me,
and holy is your name.

Right side:
Your mercy is from generation to generation
toward those who revere you.

Left side:
You have showed strength with your arm
and scattered the proud in their grandiosity.

Right side:
You have put down the mighty from their thrones
and lifted up the lowly and powerless.

Left side:
You have filled the hungry with good things
and the rich you have sent away empty.

Right side:
You, remembering your mercy, have helped your people
as you promised our ancestors, Abraham and Sarah:
Mercy to their children forever.

All:
My heart proclaims your greatness, O my God,
And my spirit rejoices in you, my Savior!

Leader:
We have joined in Mary's song of praise. Let us join Jesus
now as he prays for us and with us and within us:

All:
Our Father and Mother . . .
for the kingdom, the power and the glory are yours, now
and forever. Amen.

(Pause)

All:
Now Lord, you may let your servant go in peace,
according to your word, for my eyes have seen your sal-
     vation which you have prepared in the sight of all the
     nations,
a light of revelation to the Gentiles
and the glory of your people, Israel.

Leader:
Let us exchange a gesture of peace and then go forth to
serve the Lord.

FOLLOW-UP

A. Journaling

One of the main themes of Luke's gospel is the idea of being "on the way." Luke has marked out three stages in Jesus' journey. Each of these stages included acceptance and rejection, the valleys and the mountain tops, the decision and indecision of the crossroad—and always a firm resolve to "proceed toward Jerusalem" (9:51). In looking at your own life journey in terms of major stages, describe where you have been and where you are going. Who is with you on your journey? What experiences have taken you in different directions? Do you have a place where you can rest and pray? Have you reached out to others on the way? When have you been able to recognize the presence of Jesus "on the way"?

B. Additional Resources

1. Read as much of the gospel of Luke as you can, using the outline in Perkins, p. 232 as a guide.

2. If your Bible has an introduction to the gospel of Luke, read it.

3. Read: Anthony Marinelli, *Understanding the Gospels,* Chapter 4, "The Synoptic Gospels," pp.67-70.

4. Read: *The Catholic Study Bible,* "Luke," RG 417-437.

5. In his gospel Luke traces the spread of the gospel from Galilee to Jerusalem; in the Acts of the Apostles, he shows how the gospel spread all the way to Rome. Using the Hammond *Atlas of the Bible Lands*, find these places. Look also at Paul's missionary travels which we will study next semester.